Edward D. Andrews

THE CREATION DAYS OF GENESIS

Were the Creation Days Literally 24 Hours Long?

THE CREATION DAYS OF GENESIS

Were the Creation Days Literally 24 Hours Long?

Edward D. Andrews

Christian Publishing House
Cambridge, Ohio

Christian Publishing House
Professional Christian Publishing of the Good News

Copyright © 2015 Christian Publishing House

All rights reserved. Except for brief quotations in articles, other publications, book reviews, and blogs, no part of this book may be reproduced in any manner without prior written permission from the publishers. For information, write,

support@christianpublishers.org

Unless otherwise stated, scripture quotations are from *The Holy Bible, English Standard Version®*, copyright © 2001 by Crossway Bibles, a publishing ministry of Good News Publishers. Used by permission. All rights reserved.

THE CREATION DAYS OF GENESIS Were the Creation Days Literally 24 Hours Long?

ISBN-13: 978-0692401330

ISBN-10: 0692401334

CHAPTER 1 The Creation Days of Genesis 7

> Going Back to the Beginning 31
>
> First Day: Light (1:3–5) 33
>
> Second Day: The Expanse (1:6–8) 35
>
> Third Day (a): Land (1:9–10) 36
>
> Third Day (b): Vegetation (1:11-13) 38
>
> Fourth Day: Sun, Moon, and Stars, (1:14–19) 38
>
> Fifth Day: Sea Animals and Birds, (1:20–25) 42
>
> Sixth Day: Land Animals and Man, (1:24–31) 43

CHAPTER 2 Does the Hebrew Word for Earth at Genesis 1:1 and 1:10 Have the Same Meaning? 54

> More than One Sense 54

CHAPTER 3 Was Light Created or Made and Was It on the First Day or the Fourth Day? 57

> Created or Made – First or Fourth Creation Day 59

CHPTER 4 Is There a Different Order of Creation in Genesis 2 than Genesis 1? . 63

From Outline to Detail 63

CHAPTER 5 Who are the "us" and "our" of Genesis 1:26 65

Different Interpretations 65

CHAPTER 6 Were Adam and Eve Real Historical Persons? 67

Scriptural Evidence 67

Bibliography 69

CHAPTER 1 The Creation Days of Genesis

There are over a dozen different interpretations concerning the creative days of Genesis. Herein we will consider the main four in an effort to make our point. First, there is the *young earth view* that asserts that all physical creation was produced in just six literal 24-hour days sometime between 6,000 and 10,000 years ago. Second, there is the *day-age view* that asserts that each creative day is to be understood figuratively as creative periods of unknown durations of time. According to this view, the earth is millions of years old, and the universe is billions of years old. Third, there is the *restoration view* (gap theory) that asserts that there is a large gap of time between Genesis 1:1 and 1:2. Fourth, there is the *literary framework view* that asserts that God was not having Moses address how He created the world, nor the length of time in which to do such. This view holds that this account in Genesis 1 is merely a literary outline that summarizes a theology of creation. This so-called "seven day framework" is not to be understood in a literal sense of order and chronology, but is a literary device expressing God's involvement in creation and the Sabbath.

All four of these views are held by different Evangelical Christian scholars, but the authors of this book set aside three of these as being contrary to Scripture and science. We will discuss the first two views listed above in more detail below.[1]

We do not believe those who hold to the young-earth view of creationism have the evidence to support their case. Actually, we do not believe they even speak in terms of evidence. Why? Most of the young-earth commentators attempt to disprove the day-age view by using many words like "possibly," "could be," "may be," and so on. Also, we do not believe they look at the evidence without theological bias. Professor Kirk Wise writes:

I am a young-age creationist because that is my understanding of the Scripture. As I shared with my professors years ago when I was in college, if all the evidence in the universe turns against creationism, I would be the first to admit it, but I would still be a creationist because that is what the Word of God seems to indicate. Here I must stand. (Ashton, 2001)[2]

---

1. For a more in-depth understanding of these for creative views, see Gregory A. Boyd and Paul R. Eddy, *Across the Spectrum* (Grand Rapids, Baker Academic, 2002), 50–73.

2. http://richarddawkins.net/articles/115.

It shows theological bias when he states that no evidence will change his mind. Just as in the case of Galileo, theologians cast doubt on the Bible by ignoring scientific evidence. The Bible was not out of harmony with the truth that the earth revolves around the sun and not the other way. God's Word needed no revision. It was the Catholic Church's misinterpretation of the Bible that caused the problem. As one grows in understanding of physics, biology, and chemistry (as is also true with history, ancient languages, and manuscripts), one may need to revise conclusions derived from previous knowledge. When knowledge increases, it calls for humility to make adjustments in ones thinking.

To suggest, as do many conservative Christians, that one needs to read the Bible in a plain way (*sensus plenoir*) is quite misleading, as though one would never consider otherwise. Galileo's own words to a pupil said it well: "Even though Scripture cannot err, its interpreters and expositors can, in various ways. One of these, very serious and very frequent, would be when they always want to stop at the purely literal sense."[3] The professor argues that because Genesis chapter one was written as

---

3. Letter from Galileo to Benedetto Castelli, December 21, 1613.

historical narrative, it disallows an interpretation that has millions of years involved. This is hardly the case, for he goes on to admit that other historical narratives contain imbedded material that is not to be taken literally. Moreover, it is implied that one who accepts long creative periods must also believe the Big Bang theory, and believe that fossils are millions of years old, and believe in other facets of Evolution. This is simply untrue.

Simply put, Genesis 1:1 says: "In the beginning God created the heavens and the earth." (*ESV*) This would include our home, the earth, and our solar system and galaxy that King David referred to when he looked into the night sky and wrote: "When I look at your heavens, the work of your fingers, the moon and the stars, which you have set in place, what is man that you are mindful of him, and the son of man that you care for him?" (Psalm 8:3, 4, *ESV*) It would also include all the billions of universes that David was unable to see with his naked eye. Therefore, all this came *before* the first day of creative preparation for life on the earth that starts in Genesis 1:3, as would also be the case with the description of the earth as found in verse 2. It is not until we get to Genesis 1:3–5 that Moses starts to expound on the first day of creation specifically in respect to the earth.

What does this mean? It means that regardless of how long you may feel the creative days were, verses 1 and 2 are covering things that existed prior to the start of the events described in the successive creative days. Therefore, it takes nothing away from the Bible when geologists state that the earth is four billion years old, or astronomers who have calculated the age of the universe say it is at least 14–20 billion years old. For the Christian to argue with science is only history repeating itself, as you will see before this chapter closes. Again, Genesis chapter one, verses 1, 2, are outside the events of the creative days, which are simply a summary of the steps taken to transform the condition of verse 2 into the habitable earth in which the animals and Adam and Eve were created.

Now that we have settled the controversy between science and the *erroneous* interpretations of man's tradition that the universe and earth were created in only six literal days, we should clear the air over the age and origin of the sedimentary geological strata. Many have postulated that it was formed at the time of the flood of Noah. This answer is not to be found in God's Word. Those who hold to the young-earth view (6,000–10,000 years old), work very hard to try to reconcile the geologic column and the fossils of dinosaurs and such, in which they try to overcome evidence that shows the earth is millions of years old. What is now known and acknowledged by science is that the geological record does *not* contain a series of gradual and progressive stages of fossils from one species to another. Actually, the fossil record supports the creation account in that new species appear suddenly on the scene within this geological column, having absolutely no connection with any other species. The problem with young-earth proponents is that they are unable to use this information because it will not fit with their belief that all land and sea animals were created in two 24-hour days. This is not to say that this publication accepts the idea that the sea and land animals have existed for untold hundreds of millions of years, but it does not negate that the fifth and sixth creative days were possibly many thousands of years long, having flying and sea creatures, and land animals being created throughout, as well as dinosaurs.

What exactly does the Bible reveal? It says plainly that Jehovah God is the "fountain of life." (Psalm 36:9) In other words, life did not come from nothing, and then develop gradually in some evolutionary process over billions of years. Additionally, God's Word says that everything was created according to its kind. (Genesis 1:11, 21, 24) And finally, the Bible does provide the time period of man's creation, some 6,000 years ago. On this, both archaeology and Biblical chronology are not far off from each other. Creation is clearly stated within God's Word, and can be understood in relation to the correct study and interpretation of its texts, in light of factual science, astronomy, physics, chemistry, geology, and biology. The evolutionary theory stands in opposition to the Bible and to the facts of paleontology and biology. The ideas of young-earth creationists are not supported by God's Word either, conflicting with astronomy, physics, and geology.

Back in the seventeenth century, the world-renowned scientist Galileo proved beyond any doubt that the earth was not the center of the universe, nor did the sun orbit the earth. In fact, he proved it to be the other way around (no pun intended), with the earth revolving around the sun. However, he was brought up on charges of heresy by the Catholic Church and ordered to recant his position. Why? From the viewpoint of the Catholic Church, Galileo was contradicting God's Word, the Bible. As it turned out, Galileo and science were correct and the Church was wrong, for which it issued a formal apology in 1992. However, the point we wish to make here is that in all the controversy, the Bible was never in the wrong. It was a misinterpretation on the part of the Catholic Church, and not a fault with the Bible. One will find no place in the Bible that claims the sun orbits the earth. So where would the Church get such an idea? From Ptolemy (b. about 85 C.E.), an ancient astronomer, who argued for such an idea.

A geocentric model that the earth is the center of the universe was long held by Ptolemy's predecessors like Aristotle and most of the ancient Greek philosophers. The idea of the earth being the center of the universe was held on to by the fact that the observer with his naked eye saw both the sun and moon appear to revolve around the earth each day, while the earth appeared to stand still. Now consider that the church fathers of the third to the fifth centuries C.E. were inundated by Greek thought, believing philosophical thinking was a means of interpreting God's Word. Commenting on such ones, Douglas T. Holden[4]

---

4. Douglas T. Holden, *Death Shall Have no Dominion: A New Testament Study* (Bloomington: Bethany Press, 1971), 14.

stated, "Christian theology has become so fused with Greek philosophy that it has reared individuals who are a mixture of nine parts Greek thought to one part Christian thought." Couple this with a literal reading of some texts that should be understood figuratively and you have the makings for a conflict between the Church and the scientific world.

In interpretation, you may find one verse that appears to be in direct conflict with another (such as, the earth will be destroyed by fire, or, the earth will last forever). We do not automatically assume that God's original Word is wrong. We must do some investigative work: (1) Is there a scribal error? (2) Is there an error in translation? (3) Is this a case of one verse using "earth" in a literal sense, while another is using figurative language, speaking of mankind as the "earth?" This can be the case with science as well. One does not let the scientific world dictate our understanding of Scripture, but we should not be so dogmatic in the face of scientific facts that we will, like Professor Kirk Wise, set aside "all the evidence in the universe [that] turns against creationism," while still holding onto erroneous, unreasonable, and unscriptural interpretations.

We have many of conservative scholarship who still argues that the earth and all life on it were created in six literal 24-hour days. As you may know, this flatly contradicts modern-day science. Do we have another Galileo moment in time? Who is correct here, the scholars or science? One thing is for certain, there is no fault to be found in God's Word. The Bible does not explicitly say these creative days were literal 24-hour days. What many are failing to realize and quite a few refuse to accept is that, in both the Hebrew and the Greek Scriptures, the word for "day" (Heb., *yohm;* Gr., *hēmera*) is used both in a literal and in a figurative sense. Moreover, this is not a case of inerrancy. In other words, if one does not accept six literal 24 hour days, he has abandoned inerrancy. True inerrancy does not consider whether they are literal or figurative creative days, but rather is your interpretation in harmony with what the author meant by the words that he used.

These six creative days are representative of being like six successive days of a week. If we look at most modern translations, they read, "**the** first day," "**the** second day," "**the** third day," and so on. This is an error in translation and should read. "And there was evening and there was morning, **a** first day." (Gen. 1:5) There is no definite article in the Hebrew of these six creative days. It is the translators that choose to add it into their translations. (ESV,

LEB, HCSB, NIV, etc.) However, the American Standard Version and the New American Standard Bible read, "And there was evening and there was morning, one day." (1:5) If we were talking about a definite period of time, generally there should be a definite article in the Hebrew, because it is written in the prose genre. It is only in Hebrew poetry that the definite article could be omitted. What we are looking at with these six creative days is simply a sequential pattern, as oppose to six literal units of definite time.

SIX CREATIVE DAYS		
Day	Works	Genesis
1	Light gradually came to be;[5] a separation between day and night	1:3–5
2	Expanse, a separation between the waters	1:6–8

---

5. Many believe that God said: "Let there be light" and it immediately appeared. No, this was a gradual process, taking such an enormous amount of time that speculation would be the result of any guess. J. W. Watt's translation reflects this gradual process: "And gradually light came into existence." (*A Distinctive Translation of Genesis*) This light from our sun was spread through the dark overcast, to the point that it was not at first observable but gradually became observable through time.

	below from the waters above	
3	Dry land appears; produces vegetation	1:9–13
4	Sources of light now become visible from earth[6]	1:14–19
5	Aquatic souls and flying creatures	1:20–23
6	Land animals; man and woman created	1:24–31

While the word "day" in Hebrew can mean a 24-hour period, clearly *yohm* and context allows for the creative days to be understood as a period of time, an age, or an era. For example, immediately after he mentions the six creative days, Moses uses the same word for "day" in a more general way, lumping *all six creative days together as one day:*

---

6. And God said, "Let there be light," and there was light, the first day. Hebrew has different words that distinguish their source and their quality. The Hebrew word used in verse one for "light" is *ohr*, which carries the general sense. However, by the fourth "day," or creative period, the Hebrew word changes to *maohr*, which is now referring to the source of the light.

Genesis 2:4: These are the generations of the heavens and of the earth when they were created, in the day that Jehovah God made earth and heaven.

Here we are given the context of just how Moses is using *yohm*, which in this verse is referring to all six creative periods as "in the day." With this alone, it is difficult to argue that in chapter one *yohm* was being used to refer literally to a 24-hour period. Below are a few other examples where *yohm* is being used in the sense of an extended period of time, age, or era:

Proverbs 25:13 (*ASV*): As the cold of snow *in the time* ["day" *yohm*] of harvest, So is a faithful messenger to them that send him; For he refresheth the soul of his masters.

Isaiah 4:2 (*ASV*): *In that day* [*yohm*] shall the branch of Jehovah be beautiful and glorious, and the fruit of the land shall be excellent and comely for them that are escaped of Israel.

Zechariah 14:1 (*ASV*): Behold, *a day* [*yohm*] *of* Jehovah cometh, when thy spoil shall be divided in the midst of thee.

You will have those who cling to the 24-hour creative day by informing you that *yohm*, "day, " is used 410 times outside of Genesis with a day and number and in all cases it is to be taken literally, meaning an ordinary day. First, let us point out that there is no absolute grammatical rule in Hebrew that would make this mandatory in every case. Young-earth proponents must support their proposition with their circular argument. For the sake of an argument, let us say that their claim is true. To have "day" used with an ordinal number in 410 places outside of Genesis chapter one would not negate *yohm* being used in a different setting (like creation) with ordinal numbers and still be referring to periods of time (epochs). One must keep in mind that those uses of a *yohm* outside the creation account are used in reference to humans and a human day. Because Genesis is the only place in Scripture where periods of time can be used with ordinal numbers, there is no problem with it being the exception to the rule. No other book has the setting of the creation of heaven and earth, so to equate uses of *yohm* in totally different settings with its use in Genesis is circular reasoning, as if to say: "*Yohm* is used with ordinals in 410 occurrences outside of Genesis and they are literal, so *yohm* must be literal in Genesis because it is used with ordinal numbers." You might as well say that "*yohm* is literal with ordinal numbers because *yohm* should be literal with ordinal numbers." The young-earth proponent's argument is circular by supporting a premise with a premise instead of a conclusion.

Exodus 20:11: For in six days Jehovah made heaven and earth, the sea, and all that in them is, and rested the seventh day: wherefore Jehovah blessed the sabbath day, and hallowed it.

Is Moses, the writer of Genesis, making reference here at Exodus 20:11 to the six creative days as a representative for the weekly Sabbath, thus suggesting that the six creative days were literal 24-hour days? No, this is not so. At Genesis 2:4, the same writer uses *yohm*, "day," figuratively to refer to the six creative days of Genesis chapter one and Exodus 20:11 as a whole, starting from the gradual appearance of light on the first day (Genesis 1:3, as it would appear to an earthly observer), but does not include the earth as it lay in its prior existence, in which it is described as being "without form and void, and darkness was over the face of the deep. And the Spirit of God was hovering over the face of the waters."

Another stumbling block for those who wish to take the creation account in a literal sense of 24-hour periods is that the context is really presented as events that take long periods of time to accomplish.

Genesis 1:11, 12: And God said, Let the earth put forth grass, herbs yielding seed, and fruit-trees bearing fruit after their kind, wherein is the seed thereof, upon the earth: and it was so. [Resulting in] And the earth brought forth grass, herbs yielding seed after their kind, and trees bearing fruit, wherein is the seed thereof, after their kind: and God saw that it was good.

Obviously we are dealing with far more time than one 24-hour day would allow when speaking of grass, herbs, and fruit trees sprouting *and* growing to maturity *and* producing seed and fruit.

Genesis 2:18–20: And Jehovah God said, It is not good *that the man should be alone;* I will make him a help meet for him. And out of the ground Jehovah God formed every beast of the field, and every bird of the heavens; and brought them unto the man to see what he would call them: and whatsoever the man called every living creature, that was the name thereof. And the man gave names to all cattle, and to the birds of the heavens, and to every beast of the field; but for man there was not found a help meet for him.

At this point in the creation account it was still the sixth creative day. However as verse 27 of chapter 1 shows, it is the close of the sixth creation day. After all else had been created, after the animals had been fashioned, just before sundown of that day, "God created man in his own image, in the image of God he created him; male and female he created them." Taken literally, this means that Adam and Eve were created in the last hour of the sixth day. The question here is, if the sixth "day" was only going to be 24 hours, why would Adam be lonely? God would have known he was creating his helper in that sixth "day." Why the concern for loneliness if it were only moments before Eve was to be created? For this reader, the implication is that the sixth day is a long creative period.

Even more activity would be impossibly crammed into the sixth creative day if it were only a 24-hour period. Adam is assigned the task of naming the different kinds of animals. This is not a simple task of just picking a name randomly. In the ancient culture, names carried even more meaning than in our modern Western culture. Names were chosen to be descriptive, to reflect something about the person, animal, or thing. From the descriptive forms of the names Adam chose, it is obvious that it took some time, for the account literally reads "whatever the man called *every living creature*, that was its name."[7] (Genesis 2:19) For example, the Hebrew word for the "ass" refers to the usual reddened color. The Hebrew word for stork is the feminine form of the word meaning "loyal one."[8] This name is certainly a perfect fit, as the stork is known for the loving care it gives its young, and the loyalty of staying with its mate for life, something that would have been impossible to observe within a mere 24-hour day.

Regardless, it has been estimated, even if Adam has taken just one minute to name each pair, it would have taken 40 days with no sleep. It was only after Adam completed this task that Eve was created. Yet, even conceding the possibility that the process of naming the animals went quicker, because Adam named only the basic kinds of animals, like what went in Noah's ark at the time of the flood, which did not involve thousands of creatures, it would have taken weeks, possibly months, not a literal 24-hour day. It is during the process of Adam's

---

7. Walter A. Elwell and Barry J Beitzel, *Baker Encyclopedia of the Bible* (Grand Rapids, Mich.: Baker Book House, 1988), S. 93.

8. *Enhanced Brown-Driver-Briggs Hebrew and English Lexicon*. electronic ed. (Oak Harbor, WA : Logos Research Systems, 2000), S. 339.

naming the animals that it is discovered that "for the man no helper was found who was like him." (Genesis 2:20) Thus, we now see where the concern from Genesis 2:18 comes from, with God's reference to Adam's getting lonely. If it took weeks, months, or decades for Adam to complete his assignment of naming the animals, he would have had the time to grow lonely, but not in a couple hours as would be the case with a 24-hour day. Thus, the context here is that over a long period of time of naming the animals, Adam took note that he was alone while all the animals had mates. Let us take an extensive look at this again with the leading Hebrew language scholar of the 20th century, Dr. Gleason L. Archer.

It thus becomes clear in this present case, as we study the text of Genesis 1, that we must not short-circuit our responsibility of careful exegesis in order to ascertain as clearly as possible what the divine author meant by the language His inspired prophet (in this case probably Moses) was guided to employ. Is the true purpose of Genesis 1 to teach that all creation began just six twenty-four-hour days before Adam was "born"? Or is this just a mistaken inference that overlooks other biblical data having a direct bearing on this passage? To answer this question we must take careful note of what is said in Genesis 1:27 concerning the creation of man as the closing act of the sixth creative day. There it is stated that on that sixth day (apparently toward the end of the day, after all the animals had been fashioned and placed on the earth—therefore not long before sundown at the end of that same day), "God created man in His own image; He created them male and female." This can only mean that Eve was created in the closing hour of Day Six, along with Adam.

As we turn to Genesis 2, however, we find that a considerable interval of time must have intervened between the creation of Adam and the creation of Eve. In Gen. 2:15 we are told that Yahweh Elohim (i.e., the LORD God) put Adam in the garden of Eden as the idle environment for his development, and there he was to cultivate and keep the enormous park, with all its goodly trees, abundant fruit crop, and four mighty rivers that flowed from Eden to other regions of the Near East. In Gen 2:18 we read, "Then the LORD God said, 'It is not good for the man to be alone; I will make him a helper suitable for him.'" This statement clearly implies that Adam had been diligently occupied in his responsible task of pruning, harvesting fruit, and keeping the ground free of brush and undergrowth for a long enough period to lose his initial excitement and sense of thrill at this wonderful occupation in the beautiful paradise of Eden. He had begun to feel a certain lonesomeness and inward dissatisfaction.

In order to compensate for this lonesomeness, God then gave Adam a major assignment in natural history. He was to classify every species of animal and bird found in the preserve. With its five mighty rivers and broad expanse, the garden must have had hundreds of species of mammal, reptile, insect, and bird, to say nothing of the flying insects that also are indicated by the basic Hebrew term ʽôp̄ ("bird") (2:19). It took the Swedish scientist Linnaeus several decades to classify all the species known to European scientists in the eighteenth century. Doubtless there were considerably more by that time than in Adam's day; and, of course, the range of fauna in Eden may have been more limited than those available to Linnaeus. But at the same time it must have taken a good deal of study for Adam to examine each specimen and decide on an appropriate name for it, especially in view of the fact that he had absolutely no human tradition behind him, so far as nomenclature was concerned. It must have required some years, or, at the very least, a considerable number of months for him to complete this comprehensive inventory of all the birds, beasts, and insects that populated the Garden of Eden.

Finally, after this assignment with all its absorbing interest had been completed, Adam felt a renewed sense of emptiness. Genesis 2:20 ends with the words "but for Adam no suitable helper was found." After this long and unsatisfying experience as a lonely bachelor, God saw that Adam was emotionally prepared for a wife—a "suitable helper." God, therefore, subjected him to a deep sleep, removed from his body the bone that was closest to his heart, and from that physical core of man fashioned the first woman. Finally God presented woman to Adam in all her fresh, unspoiled beauty, and Adam was ecstatic with joy.

As we have compared Scripture with Scripture (Gen. 1:27 with 2:15–22), it has become very apparent that Genesis 1 was never intended to teach that the sixth creative day, when Adam and Eve were both created, lasted a mere twenty-four hours. In view of the long interval of time between these two, it would seem to border on sheer irrationality to insist that all of Adam's experiences in Genesis 2:15–22 could have been crowded into the last hour or two of a literal twenty-four-hour day. The only reasonable conclusion to draw is that the purpose of Genesis 1 is not to tell how fast God performed His work of creation (though, of course, some of His acts, such as the creation of light on the first day, must have been instantaneous). Rather, its true purpose was to reveal that the Lord God who had revealed Himself to the Hebrew race and entered into personal covenant relationship with them was indeed the only true God, the Creator of all things that are. This stood in direct opposition to the religious notions of the heathen around them, who assumed the emergence of pantheon of gods in successive stages out of preexistent matter of unknown origin, actuated by forces for which there was no accounting.[9]

Below, we see more examples of accounts within creation that are not instantaneous.

Genesis 2:8-9 American Standard Version (ASV)

⁸ And Jehovah God planted a garden in Eden, in the East, and there he put the man whom he had formed. ⁹ And **out of the ground made Jehovah God to grow every**

---

[9] Gleason L. Archer, New International Encyclopedia of Bible Difficulties, Zondervan's Understand the Bible Reference Series, 59-60 (Grand Rapids, MI: Zondervan Publishing House, 1982).

tree that is pleasant to the sight, and good for food; the tree of life also in the midst of the garden, and the tree of the knowledge of good and evil.

The straightforward reading of this text is that it is not an instantaneous creation. It is that Jehovah God planted the trees, and they grew as we understand trees grow, in a normal fashion.

Genesis 1:11-12 English Standard Version (ESV)

11 And God said, "Let the earth sprout vegetation, plants yielding seed, and fruit trees bearing fruit in which is their seed, each according to its kind, on the earth." And it was so. **12** The earth **brought forth vegetation**, plants yielding seed according to their own kinds, and trees bearing fruit in which is their seed, each according to its kind. And God saw that it was good.

Here again, the straight-forward reading, we are seeing the natural process of all vegetation, as opposed to it being created instantly.

In addition, it should be noted that God's Word explicitly helps man to appreciate that a "day" to Jehovah God is not measured in the same way as man.

Psalm 90:4: For in Your sight a thousand years are like yesterday that passes by, like a few hours of the night.

2 Peter 3:8: Dear friends, don't let this one thing escape you: with the Lord one day is like 1,000 years, and 1,000 years like one day.

2 Peter 3:10: But the Day of the Lord will come like a thief; on that [day] the heavens will pass away with a loud noise, the elements will burn and be dissolved, and the earth and the works on it will be disclosed.

Going Back to the Beginning

Genesis 1:1 English Standard Version (ESV)

¹ **In the beginning**, God created the heavens and the earth.

What do we learn from this one little phrase? **First**, the universe had a beginning. **Second**, since Jehovah God is the Creator of the Universe, then his existence is outside of creation, In other words, God is existing outside the material universe and so not limited by it. He is beyond, outside of his creation. **Third**, prior to the creation account of the universe, there was no matter and energy. Rather, the universe was created from nothing. **Fourth**, before Genesis 1:1 activity, there was no time as we know it. **Fifth**, God is the sovereign of the universe, and it is him alone that sets the laws and standards that exist under the umbrella of that sovereignty. The 24 elders on the Revelation of John proclaim, "Worthy are you, our Lord and God, to receive glory and honor and power, for you created all things, and by your will they existed and were created." (Rev. 4:11) It is beyond science as to how matter and energy came into existence, because what they do know by natural law (thermodynamics), 'energy cannot be created or destroyed.' All science can do is accept the matter and energy are givens. On the other hand, God's Word is clear that he supernaturally created matter, energy, space, and time as well as the laws that govern them.

Genesis 1:2 English Standard Version (ESV)

² The earth was without form and void, and darkness was over the face of the deep. And the Spirit of God was hovering over the face of the waters.

In order to deal with the scientific view that the universe is 20 billion years old, they would postulate that that time is to be found between Genesis 1:1 and 1:2. This is why in some translations, you find a space between verse 1 and verse 2, which is known as the Gap Theory (or Restitution Theory).[10] There is no reason to suggest such an idea, it is simply that God by way of his human author, Moses, informed the readers of the creation of the universe, followed by the condition of the earth, before God turn his attention to carrying out acts of creation on the earth, to prepare it for human habitation. According to verses 1 and 2, the universe, which includes the earth was in existence for an unknown period of time before God began the creative days.

First Day: Light (1:3–5)

Genesis 1:3-5 Updated American Standard Version (UASV)

³And God proceeded to say, "Let light come to be, and there came to be light. ⁴ And

---

[10] This is "as if some great catastrophe (presumably the fall of Satan and his banishment to Earth) befell Earth after its original perfect and complete creation. On this view the six days of creation actually represent the re-creation of the world after its original demise. This view is not widely supported today because it is neither consistent with the grammar of the text nor supportable from the scientific evidence. Nonetheless, it is impossible to know how much (if any) time elapsed between verses 1 and 2." (Whorton 2008)

God saw that the light was good. And God divided the light from the darkness. **⁵** God began calling the light Day, and the darkness he called Night. And there came to be evening and there came to be morning, one day.

There are many different interpretations about how long the Genesis creation days were. We are only going to concern ourselves with two, because one is the orthodox position, the other is the second most common position and the position of the author. For a discussion of the length of the Genesis day, please see the first difficulty in the Bible Difficulties in Genesis, Genesis 1:1 Is the earth only 6,000 to 10,000 years old? Are the creative days literally, only 24 hours long? Keep in mind that a different interpretation of this does not alter the inerrancy of Scripture, because it is an interpretation of Scripture, not an error in Scripture. Also, you can listen to the evidence, and make the decision for yourself.

When we look at verses 2-5 of Genesis chapter 1, we need to appreciate that this is not the birth of the sun and the moon; they were there in outer space long before that first creative day. However, they would not have been visible until this time, if one were on the earth. Now, on this first creative day, light evidently punched through the expanse that surrounded the earth, so that it would have been visible to an earthly observer, had there been one. Thus, there was now an evening and there was morning, the first day, because of the rotating earth.

Second Day: The Expanse (1:6–8)

Genesis 1:6-8 English Standard Version (ESV)

⁶ And God said, "Let there be an expanse in the midst of the waters, and let it separate the waters from the waters." ⁷ And God made the expanse and separated the waters that were under the expanse from the waters that were above the expanse. And it was so. ⁸ And God called the expanse Heaven. And there was evening and there was morning, the second day.

Some older translations like the King James Version and the American Standard Version reads "let there be a firmament." Modern translations read like the ESV above, "let there be an expanse." Bible critics tried to use the rendering "firmament" to say that the Bible writers borrowed from the creation myths, as some are picture with this "firmament" as a metal dome. However, even within the King James Version, the marginal reading is "firmament." The Hebrew word, *raqia*, for "expanse" means "to spread out, stamp, or expand."

We do not understand how the Almighty God bright this separation about, pushing the waters up from the earth, until the circle of the earth was surrounded by "waters that were above the expanse." Genesis 1:20 reads "let birds fly above the earth across the expanse of the heavens."

What took place on the second "day"? How have Bible critics tried to us the poor translation of the Hebrew word for "expanse"? What picture can you draw in your mind as God accomplished the separation of the waters from the waters?

Third Day (a): Land (1:9–10)

Genesis 1:9-10 English Standard Version (ESV)

⁹ And God said, "Let the waters under the heavens be gathered together into one place, and let the dry land appear." And it was so. ¹⁰ God called the dry land Earth, and the waters that were gathered together he called Seas. And God saw that it was good.

Again, we should not expect Moses to disclose explicit detail as to how this was accomplished. However, we can see the exercise of great power on the part of God, as we are being informed about incredible earth movements in the formation of land areas. The geologist, who studies the structure of the earth, would see verses 9-10 as a series of sudden violent catastrophes. Moses, on the other hand, indicates clear direction and control by our Creator, as he formed the earth to be inhabited.

In the book of Job, He questions God. Therefore, God takes Job to task over the creation account, by asking Job numerous questions that emphasizes the greatness of God over against man. Where was Job when the earth was created? Can job measure the earth? How is it that the earth just hangs in the sky?

Job 38:3-6 English Standard Version (ESV)

³ Dress for action like a man;
I will question you, and you make it known to me.

⁴ "Where were you when I laid the foundation of the earth?
Tell me, if you have understanding.
⁵ Who determined its measurements—surely you know!
Or who stretched the line upon it?

⁶ On what were its bases sunk,
  or who laid its cornerstone,

Third Day (b): Vegetation (1:11-13)

Genesis 1:11 English Standard Version (ESV)

¹¹ And God said, "Let the earth sprout vegetation, plants[a] yielding seed, and fruit trees bearing fruit in which is their seed, each according to its kind, on the earth." And it was so.

The light from the sun was now coming through the expanse much stronger by this time, to the point of photosynthesis, which is an absolute need to green plants. This is the process by which green plants and other organisms turn carbon dioxide and water into carbohydrates and oxygen, using light energy trapped by chlorophyll.

Fourth Day: Sun, Moon, and Stars, (1:14–19)

Genesis 1:3, 5 English Standard Version (ESV)

³And God said, "**Let there be light**," and there was light. ⁵And there was evening and there was morning, **the first day**.

Genesis 1:16, 19 English Standard Version (ESV)

¹⁶And **God made the two great lights**—the greater light to rule the day and the lesser light to rule the night—and the stars. ¹⁹And there was evening and there was morning, **the fourth day**.

In the above there appears to be a Bible difficulty, in that Genesis 1:3, 5 informs the reader that God brought about light during the first creation day, when he said: "'Let there be light,' and there was light." Then, Genesis 1:16, 19 informs the reader that "God made the two great lights" during the fourth creation day. Hence, did God create or make light on the first or fourth creation day? Before we begin to answer this difficulty, we must bear in mind that Genesis was written from a human perspective, as an earthly observer, as if he were there; not from a heavenly observation.

In looking at the fourth creation day first, we see that the "greater light" for ruling the day is our sun, and the "lesser light" for ruling the night is our moon. A further explanation of this is found at Psalm 136:7-9 (ASV): "To him that made great lights; for his loving-kindness endures forever: The sun to rule by day; for his loving-kindness endures forever; the moon and stars to rule by night; for his loving-kindness endures forever."

Returning to the first creation day, we find the expression: "let there be light." *Ohr* is the Hebrew word for light, which conveys the idea of light in a broad sense. However, for the fourth creation day, a different word is chosen, *maohr*, which refers to a source of light. Rotherham, in a footnote on "Luminaries" in the *Emphasised Bible*, says: "In ver. 3, 'ôr [*ohr*], light diffused." Then he goes on to show that the Hebrew word *maohr* in verse 14 has the sense of something "affording light." In other words, on the first creation day *ohr* (light) was spread throughout the earth's atmosphere (being diffused). To an earthly observer, had he been there: he would have not been able to discern the source of light. However, by the fourth creation day, the observer would have been able to see the *maohr* (source) of that light, as the atmosphere would have changed.

It should also be noted that Genesis 1:16 does not use the Hebrew verb bara, meaning, "create." Instead, the Hebrew verb asah is used, meaning, "make." The reason being, Genesis 1:1 informs us "God created the heavens (which would include sun, moon and stars) and the earth." In other words, the "greater light" (sun) and the "lesser light" (moon) were created long before the fourth creation day. What we have on the fourth creation day is Jehovah God "making" the "greater light" and the "lesser light" to exist in a new way with the surface of the earth and the expanse that had now dissipated even further, allowing the source of light to be seen from earth. God said, "Let there be lights in the expanse of the heavens . . ." (Gen 1:14) This being a further indication of their discernibleness. In addition, they were "to separate the day from the night. And let them be for signs and for seasons, and for days and years." These were to evidence the existence of God and draw attention to His great power, as well as lead man in numerous ways.

Those who steadfastly argue for the young earth view in light of all the evidence against the, here again, this creates a problem, because they also argue that the earth's sun was not created until the fourth day, it literally did not exist until the fourth day. Some suggest that the light from the first creation day was not from our sun but from another source, maybe a temporary light source, or the illumination of God himself. The problem with this, there literal 24 hour days for the first three days had solar days, because they see the text "there was evening and there was morning" as literal. How do you have solar days for three creation days, without our sun? If these three creative days are not defined boy our sun, then the length of those days are unclear. As you can see, this is just another monumental difficulty for those that would take the creation account to be literal, when it was not meant to be taken that way.

Fifth Day: Sea Animals and Birds, (1:20–25)

Genesis 1:20-21 English Standard Version (ESV)

20 And God said, "Let the waters swarm with swarms of living creatures [souls],[11] and let birds fly above the earth across the expanse of the heavens." **21** So God created the great sea creatures and every living creature [soul] that moves, with which the waters swarm, according to their kinds, and every winged bird according to its kind. And God saw that it was good.

The literal translations here decided to be a little more dynamic equivalent in their rendering of the Hebrew nephesh chaiyah, living soul. The term applies to the creatures in the sea, as well as the birds 'flying above the

---

[11] Heb., nephesh chaiyah, singular, "living soul"

earth across the expanse of the heavens.' This would also apply to the fossil remains of sea monsters that have been discovered in recent times. If we are to fully understand the soul, it would be best to render the Hebrew nephesh (soul) and the Greek Psyche (soul) literally.

Sixth Day: Land Animals and Man, (1:24–31)

Genesis 1:24-31 Lexham English Bible (LEB)

24 And God said, "Let the earth bring forth living creatures according to their kind: cattle and moving things, and wild animals according to their kind." And it was so. 25 So God made wild animals according to their kind and the cattle according to their kind, and every creeping thing of the earth according to its kind. And God saw that *it was* good.

26 And God said, "Let us make humankind in our image and according to our likeness, and let them rule over the fish of the sea, and over the birds of heaven, and over the cattle, and over all the earth, and over every moving thing that moves upon the earth." 27 So God created humankind in his image, in the likeness of God he created him, male and female he created them. 28 And God blessed them, and God said

to them, "Be fruitful and multiply, and fill the earth and subdue it, and rule over the fish of the sea and the birds of heaven,]and over every animal that moves upon the earth."

²⁹ And God said, "Look—I am giving to you every plant *that* bears seed which *is* on the face of the whole earth, and every kind of tree *that bears fruit*. They shall be yours as food." ³⁰ And to every kind of animal of the earth and to every bird of heaven, and to everything that moves upon the earth in which *there is* life *I am giving* every green plant as food." And it was so. ³¹ And God saw everything that he had made and, behold, *it was* very good. And there was evening, and there was morning, a sixth day.

As you can see on the sixth creation day we are introduced to the creation of both domestic and wild animals, these being in relation to what man could tame and use domestically, as opposed to what remain wild. Within this creation period was also the greatest of all creation, the creation of both man and woman. It with the creation of humans alone that it was said they were 'created in the image of God.'

Then there is the problem of the seventh day, as far as the young earth view is concerned: it never ended. There was no opening and closing, as occurred with the preceding six days; it is still in progress from the close of the sixth day, more than 6,000 years ago.

Hebrews 4:4, 5, 9–11: For somewhere He has spoken about the seventh day in this way: And on the seventh day God rested from all His works. Again, in that passage [He says], They will never enter My rest. A Sabbath rest remains, therefore, for God's people. For the person who has entered His rest has rested from his own works, just as God did from His. Let us then make every effort to enter that rest, so that no one will fall into the same pattern of disobedience.

Clearly, the context of God's Word as a whole shows the earth to be much older than 6,000+ years.

Habakkuk 3:6: He stood, and measured the earth; He beheld, and drove asunder the nations; And the *eternal mountains* were scattered; The *everlasting hills* did bow; His goings were as of old.

Micah 6:2: Hear, O ye mountains, Jehovah's controversy, and ye *enduring foundations of the earth*; for Jehovah hath a controversy with his people, and he will contend with Israel.

Proverbs 8:22, 23 (*ASV*): Jehovah possessed me in the beginning of his way, Before his works of old. I was set up from everlasting, from the beginning, Before the earth was.

The writer of Proverbs is using the age of the earth to emphasize that wisdom is much older. But if one accepts the young-earth theory (4004 B.C.E. for the creation of man),[12] when Solomon, who died shortly after 1000 B.C.E., wrote this, the earth would have been only about 3,000 years old—so not much of an emphasis.

Science has established that light travels at 186,282 miles per second. We know that it takes 100,000 years for light to cross our galaxy. We also know that it has taken hundreds of millions of years for the light of the stars we now see to reach the earth. Let us not repeat the Galileo history once more. It takes humility to learn from past experience. The Galileo conflict between science and the Church should at the very least help Christendom to avoid taking "day" as a literal 24-hour day when Scripture itself allows for another understanding; context weighs in that direction

---

12. Archbishop James Usher (1581–1656) developed a chronology of the Bible, and dated creation at 4004 B.C.E.

and science has established that the earth and the universe are far older than 6,000–10,000 years. Regardless of whether some scholars will concede to the correct understanding, this would in no way put the Bible in the wrong, for it is its interpreters who have misunderstood it. We must keep in mind that science (or the scientist) has no quarrel with the Bible: the quarrel would be with the misinterpretation of the teachers of Christendom, orthodox Jews, and others.

The website ChristianAnswers.Net concludes: "The lesson to be learned from Galileo, it appears, is not that the Church held too tightly to biblical truths; but rather that it did not hold tightly enough. It allowed Greek philosophy to influence its theology and held to tradition rather than to the teachings of the Bible. We must hold strongly to Biblical doctrine which has been achieved through sure methods of exegesis. We must never be satisfied with dogmas built upon philosophic traditions."[13] However, it is also true that science alone should not determine our interpretation, but it is to be used in a balanced way, as another source to consider.

---

13. http://www.christiananswers.net/q-eden/edn-c007.html. (Accessed January 28, 2010.)

The Copernican theory was, in fact, condemned by the theologians of the Inquisition and Pope Urban VIII. They argued that it contradicted the Bible: to be specific, Joshua's statement: "O sun, stand still . . . So the sun stood still, and the moon stopped." (Joshua 10:12, *ESV*) Of course, this is not meant to be taken literally. There are several reasonable explanations, one of which, I will give you here. Verse 13 says that "the sun stopped in the midst of heaven and did not hurry to set for about a whole day." This could simply allow for a slower movement of the earth, giving the appearance to an earthly observer that the sun and moon had stood still. As for another reasonable explanation, one Bible encyclopedia comments: "While this could mean a stopping of earth's rotation, it could have been accomplished by other means, such as a refraction of solar and lunar light rays to produce the same effect." Therefore, once more, it becomes obvious that the Bible does not contradict itself.

Let us take another look at this again with the leading apologist scholar of the 20th century, Dr. Norman L. Geisler.

PROBLEM: The Bible says that God created the world in six days (Ex. 20:11). But modern science declares that it took billions of years. Both cannot be true.

SOLUTION: There are basically two ways to reconcile this difficulty. First, some scholars argue that modern science is wrong. They insist that the universe is only thousands of years old and that God created everything in six literal 24-hour days (= 144 hours). In favor of this view they offer the following:

1. The days of Genesis each have "evening and the morning," (cf. Gen. 1:5, 8, 13, 19, 23, 31), something unique to 24-hour days in the Bible.

2. The days were numbered (first, second, third, etc.), a feature found only with 24-hour days in the Bible.

3. Exodus 20:11 compares the six days of creation with the six days of a literal work week of 144 hours.

4. There is scientific evidence to support a young age (of thousands of years) for the earth.

5. There is no way life could survive millions of years from day three (1:11) to day four (1:14) without light.

Other Bible scholars claim that the universe could be billions of years old without sacrificing a literal understanding of Genesis 1 and 2. They argue that:

1. The days of Genesis 1 could have a time lapse before the days began (before Gen. 1:3), or a time gap between the days. There are gaps elsewhere in the Bible (cf. Matt. 1:8, where three generations are omitted, with 1 Chron. 3:11-14).

2. The same Hebrew word "day" (yam) is used in Genesis 1-2 as a period of time longer than 24 hours. For example, Genesis 2:4 uses it of the whole six day period of creation.

3. Sometimes the Bible uses the word "day" for long periods of time: "One day is as a thousand years" (2 Peter 3:8; cf. Ps. 90:4).

4. There are some indications in Genesis 1-2 that days could be longer than 24 hours:

a) On the third "day" trees grew from seeds to maturity and they bore like seeds (1:11-12). This process normally takes months or years.

b) On the sixth "day" Adam was created, went to sleep, named all the (thousands of) animals, looked for a helpmeet, went to sleep, and Eve was created from his rib. This looks like more than 24 hours' worth of activity.

c) The Bible says God "rested" on the seventh day (2:2), and that He is still in His rest from creation (Heb. 4:4). Thus, the seventh day is thousands of years long already. If so, then other days could be thousands of years too.

5. Exodus 20:11 could be making a unit-for-unit comparison between the days of Genesis and a work week (of 144 hours), not a minute-by-minute comparison.

Conclusion: There is no demonstrated contradiction of fact between Genesis 1 and science. There is only a conflict of interpretation. Either, most modern scientists are wrong in insisting the world is billions of years old, or else some Bible interpreters are wrong in insisting on only 144 hours of creation some several thousand years before Christ with no gaps allowing millions of years. But, in either case it is not a question of inspiration of Scripture, but of the interpretation of Scripture (and of the scientific data).[14]

In Summary

- The Hebrew word for day that was used for the creation days of Genesis chapter 1 is the same word used at Genesis 2:4 as a

---

[14] Thomas Howe; Norman L. Geisler. *The Big Book of Bible Difficulties: Clear and Concise Answers from Genesis to Revelation* (Kindle Locations 356-375). Kindle Edition.

reference to the whole of the creative period, six days, "in the day that . . ."

- The Bible uses the word for "day" as longer periods than a 24-hour day "one day is as a thousand years." (2 Peter 3:8; Psalm 90:4)
- There are indicators within the first two chapters that we are dealing with periods longer than 24-hour days.

(1) **Third Day**: At Genesis 1:11-12, we find that trees grew from seeds to maturity, and produced seeds of their kind. This takes months, even years.

(2) **Sixth day**: We find Adam was created, went to sleep, named thousands of animals (names that indicate observation of the animals), grew lonely (looking for a helper), went to sleep, Eve was produced out of Adam's rib. This is obviously longer than 24 hours.

(3) **Seventh Day**: Genesis 2:2 informs us that God "proceeded to rest."[15] The reader will note that Hebrews 4:4 shows that God is

---

[15] Why do I have it rendered as a continuous, "proceeded to rest", when most translations read "he rested"? Heb., waiyishboth (imperfect sequential): The verb is in the imperfect state denoting incomplete or continuous action, or action in progress.

still in his rest from the ending of the six creative days. Therefore, the seventy day has been running for thousands if years thus far, which allows the other creative days to be thousands of years long.

As it usually turns out, the so-called contradiction between science and God's Word lies at the feet of those who are interpreting Scripture incorrectly. To repeat the sentiments of Galileo when writing to a pupil—Galileo expressed the same sentiments: "Even though Scripture cannot err, its interpreters and expositors can, in various ways. One of these, very serious and very frequent, would be when they always want to stop at the purely literal sense."[16] I believe that today's scholars, in hindsight, would have no problem agreeing.

---

16. Letter from Galileo to Benedetto Castelli, December 21, 1613.

CHAPTER 2 Does the Hebrew Word for Earth at Genesis 1:1 and 1:10 Have the Same Meaning?

The Hebrew word is *erets* in both verse 1 and verse 10. Erets refers to **(1)** earth, as contrasted to the heavens (Gen 1:1); **(2)** or more restricted to all the dry land of the earth (1:10); **(3)** or restricted even further by referring to just the land of a certain section of the earth (Gen 10:10); **(4)** or ground (Gen 1:26); **(5)** or people of the human race (Gen 18:25).

More than One Sense

Many people do not realize that all words have more than one sense (meaning). The context will determine which sense belongs to the use under consideration. Even if we were to consider the word "mean," we cannot ascertain what we mean by "mean" outside its context. She says she is resigning, and I think this time she *means* it, would be an expression of intention. I do not know what half these words *mean*, is indicating a particular sense. That is not quite what I *meant*, is intent. Then, let us go to what the dictionary actually considers another word but spelled the same way. You hurt her feelings, which was a *mean* thing to do. He plays a *mean* sax, which is used in the sense of being skillful. This is the *meanest* climate I have ever lived in, which means uncomfortable. Moreover, we could even look at another term, which is spelled the same but considered a different word from the first two cases of "mean." We need to find the *mean* between these extremes.

According to A Hebrew and English Lexicon of the Old Testament (Gesenius, Brown, Driver, and Briggs; 1951) erets means: "1. a. earth, whole earth ([as opposed] to a part) . . . b. earth, [as opposed] to heaven, sky . . . c. earth=inhabitants of earth . . . 2. Land = a. country, territory . . . b. district, region . . . 3. a. ground, surface of ground . . . b. soil, as productive." Old Testament Word Studies by William Wilson says of erets, "The earth in the largest sense, both the habitable and uninhabitable parts; with some accompanying word of limitation, it is used of some portion of the earth's surface, a land or country." Therefore, the first and primary meaning of the Hebrew word is our planet, or globe, the earth.

(erets) in verses 10-12 is "land," while in verses 1-2 it was "earth." Recognizing this relieves us of the problems in Paul Seely, "The Geographical Meaning of `Earth' and `Seas' in

Genesis 1:10," Westminster Theological Journal 59 (1997): 231-55, who takes [erets] as the entire earth, a flat disk of ancient conception.[17]

---

[17] C. John Collins. Genesis 1-4: A Linguistic, Literary, And Theological Commentary (Kindle Locations 3685-3687). Kindle Edition.

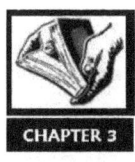

CHAPTER 3 Was Light Created or Made and Was It on the First Day or the Fourth Day?

Genesis 1:3, 5 American Standard Version (ASV)

³And God said, **Let there be light**: and there was light. ⁵And God called the light Day, and the darkness he called Night. And there was evening and there was morning, **one day**.

Genesis 1:3, 5 New American Standard Bible (NASB)

³Then God said, "**Let there be light**"; and there was light. ⁵God called the light day, and the darkness He called night And there was evening and there was morning, **one day**.

Genesis 1:3, 5 English Standard Version (ESV)

³And God said, "**Let there be light**," and there was light. ⁵And there was evening and there was morning, **the first day**.

Genesis 1:3, 5 New International Version (NIV)

³And God said, "**Let there be light**," and there was light. ⁵God called the light "day," and

the darkness he called "night." And there was evening, and there was morning—**the first day**.

Genesis 1:3, 5 Holman Christian Standard Bible (HCSB)

³Then God said, "**Let there be light**," and there was light. ⁵God called the light "day," and He called the darkness "night." Evening came, and then morning: **the first day**.

Genesis 1:16, 19 American Standard Version (ASV)

¹⁶And **God made the two great lights**; the greater light to rule the day, and the lesser light to rule the night: he made the stars also. ¹⁹And there was evening and there was morning, **a fourth day**.

Genesis 1:16, 19 New American Standard Bible (NASB)

¹⁶**God made the two great lights**, the greater light to govern the day, and the lesser light to govern the night; He made the stars also. ¹⁹There was evening and there was morning, **a fourth day**.

Genesis 1:16, 19 English Standard Version (ESV)

¹⁶And **God made the two great lights**—the greater light to rule the day and the lesser light to rule the night—and the stars. ¹⁹And there was evening and there was morning**, the fourth day**.

Genesis 1:16, 19 New International Version (NIV)

¹⁶**God made two great lights**—the greater light to govern the day and the lesser light to govern the night. He also made the stars. ¹⁹And there was evening, and there was morning—**the fourth day**.

Genesis 1:16, 19 Holman Christian Standard Bible (HCSB)

¹⁶**God made the two great lights**—the greater light to have dominion over the day and the lesser light to have dominion over the night—as well as the stars. ¹⁹Evening came, and then morning: **the fourth day**.

Created or Made – First or Fourth Creation Day

In the above there appears to be a difficulty, in that Genesis 1:3, 5 informs the reader that God brought about light during the first creation day, when he said: "'Let there be light,' and there was light." Then, Genesis 1:16,

19 informs the reader that "God made the two great lights" during the fourth creation day. Hence, did God create or make light on the first or fourth creation day? Before we begin to answer this difficulty, we must bear in mind that Genesis was written from a human perspective, as an earthly observer as if he were there; not from a heavenly observation.

In looking at the fourth creation day first, we see that the "greater light" for ruling the day is our sun, and the "lesser light" for ruling the night is our moon. A further explanation of this is found in Psalm 136:7-9 (ASV): "To him that made great lights; for his loving-kindness endures forever: The sun to rule by day; for his loving-kindness endures forever; the moon and stars to rule by night; for his loving-kindness endures forever."

Returning to the first creation day, we find the expression: "let there be light." *Ohr* is the Hebrew word for light, which conveys the idea of light in a broad sense. However, for the fourth creation day, a different word is chosen, *maohr*, which refers to a source of light. Rotherham, in a footnote on "Luminaries" in the *Emphasised Bible*, says: "In ver. 3, 'ôr ['ohr], light diffused." Then he goes on to show that the Hebrew word *maohr* in verse 14 has the sense of something "affording light." In other words, on the first creation day *ohr* (light) was spread throughout the earth's atmosphere (being diffused). To an earthly observer, had he been there: he would have not been able to discern the source of light. However, by the fourth creation day, the observer would have been able to see the *maohr* (source) of that light, as the atmosphere would have changed.

It should also be noted that Genesis 1:16 does not use the Hebrew verb bara, meaning, "create." Instead, the Hebrew verb asah is used, meaning, "make." The reason being, Genesis 1:1 informs us "God created the heavens (which would include sun, moon and stars) and the earth." In other words, the "greater light" (sun) and the "lesser light" (moon) were created long before the fourth creation day. What we have on the fourth creation day is Jehovah God "making" the "greater light" and the "lesser light" to exist in a new way with the surface of the earth and the expanse that had now dissipated even further, allowing the source of light to be seen from earth. God said, "Let there be lights in the expanse of the heavens . . ." (Gen 1:14) This being a further indication of their discernibleness. In addition, they were "to separate the day from the night. And let them be for signs and for seasons, and for days and years." These were to evidence the existence of

God and draw attention to His great power, as well as lead man in numerous ways.

CHPTER 4 Is There a Different Order of Creation in Genesis 2 than Genesis 1?

From Outline to Detail

Genesis 1:1-2 inform the reader of the creation of the heavens and the earth. **Genesis 1:3-31** gives the reader an outline of the six creative days and the basic events and creative activities on those days. **Genesis 2:1-3** is some basics on the seventh day, while **Genesis 2:4** is a summary verse of the whole six creative days. Genesis **chapter 2:5-25** is a parallel account that picks up the account, not on the first day, but the third day (after the land comes on the scene, but prior to the creation of land plants), adding details. **(2:5-6)** This chapter is used to give more details about the human creation. For example, there is no simple statement that Adam was created; it adds that he was formed out of the dust of the ground, with the breath of life being blown into him, his becoming a living soul. **(2:7)** It informs of the planting of the Garden of Eden and placing Adam in it. **(2:8)** We learn of the growth of many trees for food, tree of life, and the tree of knowledge of good and bad. **(2:9)** We are even given geographical sites that help the readers of

Moses day, to know where the Garden of Eden was. **(2:10-14)** We are told of the work assignments given to Adam, to cultivate the Garden of Eden and to name the animals. **(2:15, 19-20)** We are informed of the prohibition of eating from the tree of knowledge of good and bad. **(2:16-17)** Then, we are informed that Adam grew lonely from his naming the animals, as he saw all of them had mates. **(2:18, 20)** From there the reader gets a detailed account of the creation of Eve **(2:21-22)**, and Adam's response, with the Jehovah, in essence, performing the first marriage. **(2:23-25)** Therefore, as you can see, **chapter 1** is the barest of outlines, with **chapter 2** giving us details about the arrival of the humans. **Chapter 3:1-24** deals with the temptation of Eve by the serpent and the sinning of both Adam and Eve, with the terrible consequences of that willful rebellion.

CHAPTER 5 Who are the "us" and "our" of Genesis 1:26

Genesis 1:26-27 English Standard Version (ESV)

²⁶Then God said, "Let us make man in our image, after our likeness. And let them have dominion over the fish of the sea and over the birds of the heavens and over the livestock and over all the earth and over every creeping thing that creeps on the earth."

²⁷So God created man in his own image,

in the image of God he created him;

male and female he created them.

Different Interpretations

Different Bible scholars have offered up different interpretations over the last 2,000 years, one of which is that God is here referring to himself and the angels. However, this does not seem like a good option based on the context. If you will look at verse 26 again, you will see that God says, "Let us make man in our image" while verse 27 clearly states, "God created man in his own image," not the image of angels.

While it is true that the plural pronoun "us" is required because of the plural noun elohim (God): "Then God [*elohim*, plural] said, "Let us [plural] make man in our image." There are a couple points to keep in mind: **(1)** the plural ending "im" on elohim is majestic, expressing the majesty of God, not expressing multiple persons; **(2)** however, it is quite clear from Scripture that God's only-begotten Son was involved in the creation of man with his heavenly Father, as the Father's master worker. (John 1:3; 1:18; Col. 1:15-16; Pro. 8:21-22, 30-31, NASB) Therefore, the plural "us" and "our" simply means that two or more persons were involved. Therefore, when God used "us" and "our," he was merely addressing another person, the prehuman Jesus prior to his ascension to earth, the master workman of Proverbs 8:22-31, "the firstborn of all creation. For by him all things were created, in heaven and on earth, visible and invisible."–Colossians 1:15-16.

CHAPTER 6 Were Adam and Eve Real Historical Persons?

Critical Scholars either consider Adam and Eve as a myth or symbolic persons, representing humankind. The evidence from the Bible, on the other hand is that they are real historical persons. Before looking at the biblical evidence, let us note that Hebrew manuscripts are archaeological evidence that give us the historicity of humanity. The oldest manuscripts date to the 3rd century BC. In addition, Greek New Testament manuscripts give us how Jewish Christians from the first century, as well as the Son of God views the Hebrew Old Testament and the historicity of Adam and Eve, and these NT MSS are archaeological evidence, dating as early as the second century AD.

Scriptural Evidence

(1) Genesis 1-2 is a historical narrative that expounds on Adam and Eve's creation and events within their lives. **(2)** They are recorded as giving birth to children, as do the others mentioned in the early genealogies. (Gen 4:1, 25; 5:1) **(3)** The Hebrew word toledoth, often translated "generations," should be translated "history" at Genesis

2:4;5:1; 6:9; 10:1; 11:10; as well as five other places in Genesis. Regardless, it shows that toledoth is used all throughout Genesis, in speaking of descendants of so-and-so, and has the same meaning in its use with Adam and Eve at Genesis 5:1. **(4)** If we look at the chronologies throughout the Old Testament, Adam starts the list. (1 Chron 1:1) **(5)** All early humankind did not father Seth. No, Adam fathered him at the specific age of 130 years. (Gen 5:3) **(6)** Luke places Adam at the start of human history. (Lu 3:38) **(7)** Jesus viewed Adam and Eve as real historical persons. (Matt 19:24-25) **(8)** The inheritance of sin and death came from a literal Adam. (Rom 5:12-14) **(9)** Jesus is contrasted with Adam, which means if we deny Adam as a historical person, we deny Jesus Christ and his sacrifice as well. (1 Cor 15:45-47) **(10)** Again, Paul comes to the stage as a witness, when he informs us that Adam was created first and then Eve. (1 Tim 2:13-14) **(11)** Was Enoch the seventh in line from all early humankind? (Jude14) Reasonably, humankind had to of started from just two people at some time. The fact is that the Bible, as a reliable book and archaeological evidence of human history, gives us those two people, Adam and Eve.

Bibliography

Archer, Gleason L. *Encyclopedia of Bible Difficulties.* Grand Rapids: Zondervan, 1982.

Boyd, Gregory A, and Paul R Eddy. *Across the Spectrum.* Grand Rapids: Baker Academic, 2002.

Brown, Francis, Samuel Rolles Driver, and Charles Augustus Briggs. *Enhanced Brown-Driver-Briggs Hebrew and English Lexicon* . Oak Harbor: Logos Research Systems, 2000.

Collins, John. *Genesis 1-4: A Linguistic, Literary, and Theological Commentary.* Philipsburg: P&R, 2006.

Davis, John J. *Paradise to Prison: Studies in Genesis.* Salem: Sheffield, 1975.

Elwell, Walter A. *Baker Encyclopedia of the Bible.* Grand Rapids: Baker Book House, 1988.

Geisler, Norman L., and Thomas Howe. *The Big Book of Bible Difficulties.* Grand Rapids: Baker Books, 1992.

Holden, Douglas T. *Death Shall have no Dominion: A New Testament Study.* Bloomington: Bethany Press, 1971.

Kass, Leon R. *The Beginning of Wisdom: Reading Genesis.* New York: Free Press, 2003.

Kissling, Paul J. *The College Press NIV commentary: Genesis.* Joplin, MO: College Press Pub. Co., 2004.

Language, John Peter. *A Commentary on the Holy Scriptures: Genesis.* Bellingham: Logos Research Systems, 1939, 2008.

Longman III, Tremper. *How to Read Genesis.* Downers Groves, IL: Intervarsity Press, 2005.

Mathews, K. A. *The New American Commentary vol. 1A, Genesis 1-11:26 .* Nashville: Broadman & Holman Publishers, 2001.

Morris, Henry M. *The Genesis Record: A Scientific and Devotional Commentary on the Book of the Beginnings.* Grand Rapids: Baker Books, 2007, 1976.

Walton, John H. *Zondervan Illustrated Bible Backgrounds Commentary (Old Testament) Volume 1: Genesis, Exodus, Leviticus, Numbers, Deuteronomy.* Grand Rapids, MI: Zondervan, 2009.

www.ingramcontent.com/pod-product-compliance
Lightning Source LLC
Chambersburg PA
CBHW031420040426
42444CB00005B/658